THE ABC'S OF EFFECTIVE PRAYER

A GUIDEBOOK FOR PERSONAL PRAYER

B. T. PRINCE, JR.

Xulon
PRESS

www.xulonpress.com

SPECIAL ACKNOWLEDGEMENT

No worthwhile product is forthcoming without a process. Processes are a banding together of God-given talents enthusiastically and cooperatively in an effort to move a thought into reality. I am deeply grateful for the tremendous and loving assistance of Bible study and High School English teacher and long-time friend, Mrs. Dwain Bouldin, as well as my wonderful and very talented daughter-in-law Angela both of whom spent tireless hours in careful examination of the manuscript to assure ease of understanding and fluent transition, not to mention ferreting out and correcting many typographical thorns that always seem so eager to hide among the roses.

DEDICATION

I dedicate this book to my mother, the late Alice Turner Prince (1891 – 1976), a devout Christian, who demonstrated the importance of prayer early in my childhood and continued to live *a life that prays* until God called her home.

I also dedicate this book to the many people who experience problems with expressing themselves in prayer either alone or in front of others. May the practical thoughts expressed herein bring them to a better understanding of the mechanics of prayer and consequently a greater eagerness to go to the Lord in a true spirit of love and enthusiasm.

TABLE OF CONTENTS

THE ABC'S OF EFFECTIVE PRAYER

⌒

Many great books have been written on the subject of prayer. Although it is the superlative method of worship and is the greatest way to bring down from heaven God's abundant blessings, it is an exercise in which many people have yet to reach a point of comfort or maturity. We are told in Romans 8:26, *"Likewise, the Spirit also helps in our weaknesses. For we do not know what to pray for as we ought, but the Spirit Himself makes intercession for us with groanings which cannot be uttered."* I have long considered addressing this issue while telling myself that it would certainly get lost in the volumes of great instructional material already on the shelves. Nevertheless, the desire has not diminished, so I will attempt to outline a simple application for effective and expectant prayer. I am constantly reminded of James 5:16b which reads, *"The effective, fervent prayer of a righteous man avails much."* I certainly want my prayers to bring forth great bounty from above, and I'm sure you do also.

Prayer is basically a way to place our desires before God in total submissiveness to His will. The following acrostic identifies the goal that we are trying to accomplish:

P - Persistently
R - Reaching
A - Above
Y - Your
E - Earthly
R - Restraints

Philippians 4:6-7 speaks to this: *"Be anxious for nothing, but in everything, by prayer and supplication, with thanksgiving, let your requests be made known to God; and the peace of God which surpasses all understanding will guard your hearts and minds through Christ Jesus."*

We are exhorted to pray. First Timothy 2:1-2 says, *"Therefore, I exhort first of all that supplications, prayers, intercessions, and giving of thanks be made for all men, for kings and all who are in authority, that we may lead a quiet and peaceable life in all godliness and reverence."* Prayer is not optional for the Christian. When Jesus is speaking to His disciples about prayer in Matthew Chapter 6, He says, *"and when you pray"* not *"if you pray."* Moreover, we are urged to *"pray without ceasing"* (1 Thes. 5:17). Prayer is extremely powerful. It is one sure way of rendering Satan helpless. He can cope with most things, but he is rendered powerless by the presence of prayer.

Prayer is a lifeline to God. It is absolutely essential for spiritual health and growth. There are many aspects of effective prayer that should be carefully considered. Let us take a look at several of them.

ATTITUDE

People frequently come to me for prayer with a somewhat futile or even antagonistic attitude. Some are angry with God for allowing them to be in the situation they are facing and wonder why they are embroiled in such seemingly inescapable circumstances. They feel their value as a believer is being questioned. They have a strong desire for relief. They feel hopeless to pray and express a need for someone with a "better connection" to God to intercede for them. These attitudes interfere with effective prayer.

A proper attitude is absolutely essential in making an appearance before the throne of grace. Colossians 3:2 tells us *"to set our minds on things above, not on things on the earth."* If and when you feel your attitude is less than it should be, begin your prayer with a plea for help in getting your heart fixed on Him. Ask Him to reassure you of the truth of His word. Ask Him to draw your heart close to His. Ask Him to help you feel the touch of His hand. In such times of spiritual turmoil, it is also good to ask God to create in you a new heart and to renew a steadfast spirit within you (Psalm 51:10).

ANTICIPATION

Too often we approach prayer obligatorily. However, as described in Psalm 100, we should approach God joyfully, with gladness, with singing, with thanksgiving, and with praise. An air of excitement should be present when we go before His Majesty. Psalm 100:5 reminds us that *"the Lord is good; His mercy is everlasting, and His truth endures to all generations."* As we avail ourselves of the opportunity of coming before our loving Heavenly Father, we should look forward with delight in being able to approach Him and to receive the wonderful blessings available. It is also good to be reminded that *"God will supply all your need according to His riches in glory by Christ Jesus"* (Phil. 4:19).

APPROACHING GOD

W e need to show proper respect for the One to whom our requests are being directed. First of all, we need to go to Him with reverence and adoration for who He is. He is the Lord of Lords and the King of Kings.

"Yes, all kings shall fall down before Him; all nations shall serve Him" (Psalm *72:11).*

"Therefore God also has highly exalted Him and given Him the name which is above every name, that at the name of Jesus every knee should bow, of those in heaven, and of those on earth, and of those under the earth, and that every tongue should confess that Jesus Christ is Lord to the glory of God the Father" (Phil. *2:9-11).*

People often wonder if you have to be in any particular physical position to pray in order to show proper reverence. While it is certainly good to humble yourself before the Almighty God by bowing before Him, it is the position of the heart that matters more than the position of the body. Wherever we are, we can always bow before Him in our hearts to show our deference to His holiness. First Peter 3:12 reminds us that *"the eyes of the LORD are on the righteous, and His ears are open to their prayers; but the face of the LORD is against those who do evil."*

Secondly, we need to recognize the awesomeness of His capabilities. After all, the psalmist has said, *"The earth is the LORD's and all its fullness, the world and those who dwell therein"* (Psalm 24:1). Limitations are totally inappropriate in considering His love, His mercy, His compassion, His grace, and His undeniable ability to do whatever He chooses to do. The Apostle Paul reveals his appreciation of the revelation of God's grace in Ephesians 3:14-15: *"For this reason, I bow my knees to the Father of our Lord Jesus Christ from whom the whole family in heaven and earth is named."*

ACKNOWLEDGE

We must *acknowledge* His blessings. Psalm 36:7 says, "*How precious is Your lovingkindness, O God! Therefore, the children of men put their trust under the shadow of Your wings.*" Psalm 68:19 adds "*Blessed be the Lord who daily loads us with benefits, the God of our salvation!*" In Psalm 86:15 we read, "*But You, O Lord, are a God full of compassion, and gracious, longsuffering, and abundant in mercy and truth.*"

ASK IN JESUS' NAME

Matthew 7:7-11 tells us, *"Ask, and it will be given to you; seek, and you will find; knock, and it will be opened to you. For everyone who asks receives, and he who seeks finds, and to him who knocks, it will be opened. Or what man is there among you who, if his son asks for bread, will give him a stone? Or if he asks for a fish, will he give him a serpent? If you then, being evil, know how to give good gifts to your children, how much more will your Father who is in heaven give good things to those who ask Him!"*

As a salesman for many years, I often had the opportunity to observe other salesmen as they made their sales presentation to potential buyers. Often salesmen would be able to establish good relationships with buyers and generate genuine interest but would not be able to close the deal. Why? They simply never *asked* for the order. I learned quickly the success of the mission for which I was sent was predicated upon my asking for the commitment. James 4:2c reminds us, *"You do not have because you do not ask.*" In addition, John 14:13-14 encourages us to *ask* in Jesus' name; "*And whatever you ask in My name, that I will do, that the Father may be glorified in the Son. If you ask anything in My name, I will do it.*"

AWARENESS OF HIS PRESENCE
AND HIS WILL

Too many times, we are so engrossed in our own desires that we allow no room for re-direction. We need a special awareness of His presence that will not only give us confidence but will also reveal His will. As a result, our heart's desire will be changed to conform to His will. The first thing I had to learn was to concomitantly *pray and think in God's perfect will*. James 4:15 tells us, *"Instead, you ought to say, if the Lord wills, we shall live and do this or that."* After determining, to the best of my ability, that I am in God's will, I can pray with great confidence. It is neither the exactitude of the request nor the associated eloquence that brings forth a desired response but rather a genuine need with an unselfish purpose. We need to understand that God's perfect will must have preeminence.

BE BOLD

Another consideration in preparation for and execution of effective prayer is found in Hebrews 4:16 stating, *"Let us therefore come boldly to the throne of grace that we may obtain mercy and find grace to help in time of need."* A half-hearted prayer generally produces minimal results. If you really feel that your request is honoring to Him, then go for it without hesitation. As the old saying goes, "Make sure you are right, and then forge ahead." God will certainly not be coerced into doing anything He does not wish to do, but He does want us to come forward without hesitation.

BE EXPECTANT

One thing I've noticed over the years is that people who receive affirmative responses to prayer always seem to possess a sense of *expectancy*. Someone commented to me years ago that I prayed as though I expected God to answer my requests, and I readily admitted to such an *expectation*. Indeed, God wants us to come to Him *expectantly*.

> *"If any of you lacks wisdom, let him ask of God, Who gives to all liberally and without reproach and it will be given to him. But let him ask in faith, with no doubting, for he who doubts is like a wave of the sea driven and tossed by the wind. For let not that man suppose that he will receive anything from the Lord; he is a double-minded man, unstable in all his ways"* (James 1:6-8).

In Matthew Chapter 8, we read the story of the leper who came before Jesus expectantly with a desire to be healed.

"And behold, a leper came and worshiped Him, saying, 'Lord, if You are willing, You can make me clean.' Then Jesus put out His hand and touched him, saying, 'I am willing; be cleansed.' immediately, his leprosy was cleansed" (Matt. 8:2-3).

We need to remember that even though God can respond immediately, He doesn't always do so. Having a sense of expectancy doesn't necessarily imply having an expectation of an immediate response. Sometimes, He does not come right out and say "yes" but allows me to wait for His timing. Over the years I have learned that His timing is always better than mine. On those occasions when trying to run ahead of Him, I get the strong feeling that what I am asking for is not the best solution.

BE FORGIVING

When we go before the Father, we need to do so with clean hands and pure hearts. If God, whose hatred of sin is far beyond our ability to grasp, can forgive us for the sins we have committed, shouldn't we be able to forgive others for sins they have committed against us? Nothing anyone has ever done to us could be worse than what our sin did to God. He has told us in Matthew 18:15, *"Moreover, if your brother sins against you, go and tell him his fault between you and him alone. If he hears you, you have gained your brother."* Harboring an unforgiving spirit is sinful, and sin has a way of blocking our communication with God.

In Matthew 18 we read the story of the unforgiving servant. There was a certain servant who owed an extraordinary debt to his master. When the master tried to collect the debt from the servant and found out the servant couldn't pay him back, he ordered that the servant, his wife, and his children and all their possessions be sold in order to pay the debt. The servant pleaded with his master to have patience with him and promised to repay the debt. The master showed him compassion and forgave him the debt.

The story continues with the first servant seeking out a second servant who owed him a very small amount and demanding immediate payment. The second servant did not have the means to repay the debt, so he asked the first servant to have patience with him, and he promised he would pay back the debt. The first servant showed him no compassion but instead had him thrown in prison. Other servants who witnessed the incident went to the first servant's master and told him what the first servant had done to the second servant. The master became angry with the first servant for his lack of compassion to the second servant and had him imprisoned until he repaid his debt. The story concludes with the following warning: *"So My heavenly Father also will do to you if each of you, from his heart, does not forgive his brother his trespasses"* (Matthew 18:35).

BE GRATEFUL

All too often, when we receive an affirmative response to a prayer, we go immediately into another request or into some other activity without taking the time to stop and give Him thanks. In Luke 17, we read the story of Jesus who, as He passed through a certain village on His way to Jerusalem, met ten lepers.

> *"And they lifted up their voices and said, 'Jesus, Master, have mercy on us!' So when He saw them, He said to them, 'Go show yourselves to the priests.' And so it was that as they went, they were cleansed. And one of them, when he saw that he was healed, returned, and with a loud voice glorified God, and fell down on his face at His feet, giving Him thanks. And he was a Samaritan. So Jesus answered and said, 'Were there not ten cleansed? But where are the nine? Were there not any found who returned to*

give glory to God except this foreigner?'"
(Luke 17:13-19).

Before beginning to list our desires, we need
to pause and reflect with gratitude upon answers
already received. First Thessalonians 5:18 tells us,
*"In everything give thanks; for this is the will of
God in Christ Jesus concerning you."* This does not
say to be thankful **for** everything but **in** everything.
According to Romans 8:28, *"We know that all things
work together for good to those who love God, to
those who are the called according to His purpose."*
How truly encouraging these words are! What joy
fills our heart when we know that our simple but
genuine prayer of concern has come before the Lord
and that He has responded in an affirmative and
miraculous way.

BE HUMBLE

S o many times, people attempt to maneuver God to their way of thinking. We should quickly recognize that any such attempt can accomplish nothing. However, when we approach Him with *humility*, it greatly increases our chance of His affirmative response to our requests. In 1 Peter 5:5b-6, we read, *"Yes, all of you be submissive to one another, and be clothed with humility, for God resists the proud, but gives grace to the humble."* Frequently, I hear people trying to tell God how to answer their prayers. This is the antithesis of *humility*. We are told in Isaiah 65:24, *"It shall come to pass that before they call, I will answer; and while they are still speaking, I will hear."* Since He knows all things, it seems logical that before we come to Him, He is already considering our requests.

When the disciples began to argue about who would be the greatest in the Kingdom of Heaven, Jesus said to them, *"Therefore, whoever humbles himself as this little child is the greatest in the Kingdom of Heaven"* (Matthew 18:4). This is a beautiful portrayal of the humility we need to embrace in our prayers. Psalm 147:6a tells us, *"The Lord lifts up the humble."* Furthermore, in 1 Peter 5:6 we read, *"Therefore, humble yourselves under the mighty hand of God, that He may exalt you in due time."*

BE LOVING

Christianity is founded on love – God's overwhelming love for us. *Love* is a hallmark of our faith. In John 13: 34-35, Jesus tells His disciples "*A new commandment I give to you, that you love one another; as I have loved you, that you also love one another. By this all will know that you are My disciples, if you have love for one another.*" Prayer, therefore, should also be founded on *love*. Without love, our whole cause would be discolored. Therefore, our prayers should be sent heavenward wrapped securely in *love*. In First Corinthians 13:1 and 13, we read, "*Though I speak with the tongues of men and of angels, but have not love, I have become sounding brass or a clanging cymbal. . . . And now abide faith, hope, love, these three; but the greatest of these is love.*"

BE OBEDIENT

Obedience is essential in our Christian life. The commands God gives us throughout Scripture are designed to protect us, to help us to grow spiritually, and to help us live an abundant life. We are told in Luke that *"His mercy is on those who fear Him"* (Luke 1:50). Nevertheless, He places an obligation on us to keep our lives in order while reminding us that *"He will have mercy and compassion on whomever He elects"* (Romans 9:15). In Matthew 5:16 we read, *"Let your light so shine before men that they may see your good works and glorify your Father in heaven."* How does your life glorify the Father? Are you putting off things you know you need to do? James 4:17 says, *"Therefore, to him who knows to do good and does not do it, to him it is sin."* We have all heard that saying that procrastination is just delayed disobedience. Do you reward those who disobey or defy you? Do you really expect God to unload blessings upon you while you are in disobedience?

BE PATIENT

W hen we pray, it is very important that we exercise *patience*. So often we allow ourselves, in our human frailty, to fall victim to the very undesirable characteristic of impatience. In James 1:2-4, we are exhorted in this way, *"My brethren, count it all joy when you fall into various trials, knowing that the testing of your faith produces patience. But let patience have its perfect work that you may be perfect and complete, lacking nothing." Patience* cannot be gained overnight. However, we refuse to allow nature to take its normal course. We want *patience,* and we want it immediately. How often does God permit things to enter our lives for the express purpose of teaching us the importance of *patience*? In Romans 12:12 we are encouraged *to "Rejoice in hope, be patient in tribulation, and continue steadfastly in prayer."* God always follows his own timetable, and quite frequently His timetable varies from ours. We need to practice allowing Him to work things out according to His master plan and to remember that He has a definite plan for our lives. We need to remember His promises in Jeremiah 29:11-13:

"For I know the thoughts that I think toward you, says the LORD, thoughts of peace and not of evil to give you a future and a hope. Then you will call upon Me and go and pray to Me, and I will listen to you. And you will seek Me and find Me, when you search for Me with all your heart."

BE PERSISTENT

J ust as we must be patient and learn to wait on God's timing, we must also be *persistent*. These two traits go hand in hand. We must not give up too soon. In Luke 11:5 we read, "*And He said to them, 'Which of you shall have a friend, and go to him at midnight and say to him, Friend, lend me three loaves; for a friend of mine has come to me on his journey, and I have nothing to set before him; and he will answer from within and say, 'Do not trouble me; the door is now shut, and my children are with me in bed; I cannot rise and give to you?' I say unto you, though he will not rise and give to him because he is his friend, yet because of his persistence he will rise and give him as many as he needs.*"

We may not receive what we ask for the first time. However, that does not necessarily mean that we won't eventually receive it. We may just have to wait until the timing is right. As long as we believe that what we are asking is in accordance with His will, we should continue to bring our requests before Him. If we continue to pray without results, we may need to pause and seek God's direction. There just might be something in our life that needs correcting.

BE SPECIFIC

Too often we tend to pray general prayers such as "Lord, bless the missionaries." This type of praying is not wrong; however, praying more specifically tends to have greater effectiveness. Jesus, Himself, modeled being specific. So often He spoke asking, "What would you have me do?" He had things to do and places to go, so He went right to the question. Then, upon receiving a response, He handled the matter straightforwardly. Two examples of this are listed below:

"When Jesus departed from there, two blind men followed Him, crying out and saying, 'Son of David, have mercy on us!' And when He had come into the house, the blind men came to Him. And Jesus said to them, 'Do you believe that I am able to do this?' They said unto Him, 'Yes, Lord.' Then He touched their eyes saying, 'according to your faith, let it be to you'" (Matt. 9:27-29).

"Now a certain man was there who had an infirmity thirty-eight years. When Jesus saw him lying there and knew that he already had been in that condition a long time, He said to him, 'Do you want to be made well?' The sick man answered Him, 'Sir, I have no man to put me into the pool when he water is stirred up, but while I am coming, another steps down before me.' Jesus said to him, `Rise, take up your bed, and walk.' And immediately the man was made well, took up his bed, and walked" (John 5:5-9).

As in the case of the man with the infirmity, people often want to include all the details of a situation when praying. We must remember that, as an all-knowing God, He is already aware of the circumstances. In the above story, Jesus already knew that the man with the infirmity had been in that condition a long time. He wasn't asking the man why he didn't go down to the pool. He already knew the man's situation. He simply wanted to know if the man wanted to be made well.

BE TRUSTING

Everyday we do hundreds of things that involve trust without even thinking about it. We trust that when we flip a light switch, the light will come on. We trust that when we turn the key in the ignition of our car, the motor will start. We trust that when we go to an ATM machine and we let go of our debit card, it will go into the slot and return to us along with the amount we have requested. We do not analyze these things and wonder if they will happen. We simply trust that they will.

In our life and in our prayers, it is absolutely essential that we trust God. He is the giver of every good gift and every perfect gift (James 1:17). We need to trust His character, His abilities, His love for us, and the truth and power of His word. In Isaiah 26, we are exhorted to trust in the Lord forever. Verse three reminds us that God will keep us in perfect peace when our minds are focused on Him. In Psalm 37:3-5, we are reminded, *"Trust in the LORD, and do good; dwell in the land, and feed on His faithfulness. Delight yourself also in the LORD, and He shall give you the desires of your heart. Commit your way to the LORD, trust also in Him, and He shall bring it to pass."* You may recall that in Acts 11:12, when Peter was summoned by the Holy Spirit to go to Caesarea to speak with Cornelius, he was told to go down and go with the three men, *"doubting nothing."* In that Peter was able to lead Cornelius and others to accept Christ, it shows the reward of his trust by going as directed rather than waiting and questioning.

COMMITMENT

Prayer is a *commitment* of the highest order. Just brushing over a few items when it is convenient does not call down from heaven the abundant blessings that are available. Our *commitment* should be at the very core of our thoughts. Throughout the Bible, we are exhorted to *commit* to prayer. Luke 18:1b tells us that "*men always ought to pray and not lose heart.*" In Ephesians Chapter 6, after being urged to be strong in the Lord and to take up the whole armor of God, we are further exhorted to pray "*always with all prayer and supplication in the Spirit, being watchful to this end with all perseverance and supplication for all the saints*" (Ephesians 6:18).

CONFESS

In Psalm 66:18, we read *"If I regard iniquity in my heart, the Lord will not hear."* In view of this, we know that our first prerequisite to having our prayers answered is having a personal relationship with the Father by accepting His precious gift of eternal life. Secondly, we have to make sure that nothing is hindering our fellowship with the Father. Unconfessed sin blocks our fellowship with Him. *Confession* often brings a beautiful feeling of release and helps restore our fellowship with Him. God is a forgiving Father. First John 1:9 tells us, *"If we confess our sins, He is faithful and just to forgive us our sins and to cleanse us from all unrighteousness."* Psalm 32:5 says, *"I acknowledged my sin to You, and my iniquity I have not hidden. I said, 'I will confess my transgressions to the Lord,' and You forgave the iniquity of my sin."*

In the story of the prodigal son found in Luke 15:11-31, we find a loving father running to meet his repentant son who had returned home. He then had his servants bring out a robe that was to be put on his son and a ring to be put on his son's finger. The father then gave instructions to kill the fatted calf to celebrate his son's return. In what better way could we relate more appropriately to obtaining good things from a special kind of Father who is certainly superior to our earthly father in depth of love and abundant resources from which to draw?

COMPASSION

The subject of compassion is discussed many times in the Bible. Mark 6:34 describes the compassion of Jesus by pointing out, *"And Jesus, when He came out, saw a great multitude and was moved with compassion for them, because they were like sheep not having a shepherd. So He began to teach them many things."* In Luke 15:20, we read of the *compassion* a father showed to his prodigal son who had returned. In Luke 10:30-36, we read of the *compassion* of the Good Samaritan. In 1 Peter 3:8, we are instructed, *"Finally, all of you be of one mind, having compassion for one another; love as brothers, be tenderhearted, be courteous."* Later, in 1 John 3:17, we are told, *"But whoever has this world's goods and sees his brother in need, and shuts up his heart from him, how does the love of God abide in him?"* From this, it is easy to see that effective prayer must include *compassion* for our fellowman.

CONTINGENCIES

od gives to us out of His abundant grace. Blessings are not something we can earn. However, blessings can be, and often are, contingent upon our obedience to God. John 15:7 says, *"If you abide in Me, and My words abide in you, you will ask what you desire, and it shall be done for you."* In 1 John 3:22, we read, *"And whatever we ask we receive from Him, because we keep His commandments and do those things that are pleasing in His sight."* First John 5:14 tells us, *"Now this is the confidence that we have in Him, that if we ask anything according to His will, He hears us."* Conversely, we are told in Psalm 66:18, *"If I regard iniquity in my heart, the Lord will not hear."* From these verses it is clear that receiving affirmative answers to our prayers is definitely dependent on our obedience to God and to our abiding in Him.

CYCLE OF PRAYER

S ometimes prayer does not begin with us. Frequently it begins with God Himself. Dr. Wayne Poplin, Senior Minister, Carmel Baptist Church, Matthews, N. C., points out that prayer can be a cycle begun in heaven. How many times do we hear that "still, small voice" calling to us to lift someone in prayer? I have heard stories of mothers being awakened in the night with the conviction to pray for a child. Later, they found that a very real emergency existed at that exact hour when they were awakened and felt compelled to pray.

One great example of a cycle of prayer beginning in heaven is found in James 5:14-16.

"Is anyone among you sick? Let him call for the elders of the church, and let them pray over him, anointing him with oil in the name of the Lord. And the prayer of faith will save the sick, and the Lord will raise him up. And if he has committed sins, he will be forgiven. Confess your trespasses to one another and

*pray for one another that you may be healed.
The effective, fervent prayer of a righteous
man avails much."*

I recall going with the deacons of our church and
anointing a sister with oil in the name of the Lord
and praying over her. Her death a few weeks later
was exceedingly disturbing to me. Had I misun
derstood what was written in James? Did it not say
that if someone who was sick called on the elders
of the church to anoint him/her with oil and pray
over that person in faith that the Lord would save
the sick person? I went earnestly to the Lord for an
answer concerning this. I learned that the elders were
not called upon to pray for her, but the process had
been initiated on earth with the deacon chairman. My
distress was thereby relieved, and I quickly regained
my strong belief in the truths outlined in these scripture verses. It is good to have the deacons and/or
elders pray for anyone at any time, but when the
cycle does not begin with God, the results may be
less definitive. If it is not God's will to heal a person,
then the person will not be healed.

WHY, WHEN, & HOW OFTEN DO WE PRAY?

Three frequently asked questions concerning prayer are:

(1) Why should we pray?
(2) When should we pray?
(3) How often should we pray?

Since the answers to these questions have already been touched on throughout the discussions on the various elements of prayer, I will offer only a short recap here.

As for the "why," the answer is, of course, because Scripture urges us to pray. *"Therefore, I exhort first of all, that supplications, prayers, intercessions, and giving of thanks be made for all men, for kings and all who are in authority, that we may lead a quiet and peaceable life in all godliness and reverence."* (1 Tim.2:1-2). In Jeremiah 33:3, the Lord says to Jeremiah, *"'Call to Me, and I will answer you and show you great and mighty things which you do not know.'"* Isaiah urges us to *"Seek the LORD while He may be found, call upon Him while He is near"* (Isaiah 55:6).

As for "when" we are to pray, the answer is, of course, often. Psalm 55:17 says, *"Evening and morning and at noon I will pray, and cry aloud, and He shall hear my voice."* As for "how often," the answer is, of course, "without ceasing" (1 Thess. 5:17). Our thoughts should constantly be on His goodness and His mercy which are ever present. We should always recognize that, as a merciful God, He wants to bless us and is always open to our prayers.

We are both encouraged and reassured when we recognize that God is always looking down upon us. Psalm 34:15 tells us, *"The eyes of the Lord are on the righteous, and His ears are open to their cry."* In Psalm 50:15, we read, *"Call upon Me in the day of trouble; I will deliver you, and you shall glorify Me."* When we develop the right relationship with our Lord, realizing that we are invited to cast all of our care upon Him because He cares for us (1 Peter 5:7), we should be anxious to submit ourselves to His wonderful mercies and His abundance of grace. We know that *"He will never leave us nor forsake us"* (Hebrews 13:5).

I recall an incident that occurred when I was a young boy. My mother was very ill, and my father, knowing the closeness I shared with my mother, did not want me to know the true status of her health. He called my older siblings into a meeting and very firmly stated that I was not to be told about her condition. He did not know that I was lurking nearby and that I heard every word he said. He told my siblings that he had just come from the hospital and that the doctors told him they had exhausted all their knowledge and that nothing could keep my mother alive for longer than another twenty-four hours. I promptly went to my bedside, and in probably the most earnest prayer I have ever prayed, I simply asked God to heal my mother, to please not let my mother die. Well, my mother died about thirty-five years later, and no one except God and I knew what had taken place that day. I absolutely could not have been any more sincere or more direct. My prayer went right to the issue at hand without any doubt as to whether He could or would respond affirmatively. (Fortunately, God knows our heart.)Recently, I was told of an occasion in a nearby town where a young autistic boy wandered from his home in his pajamas. It was late evening, and darkness was setting in. Word spread quickly throughout the neighborhood, and many people went out to help search for him. One mother, unable to join in the search effort because she had to watch her two young daughters, decided that she and her daughters could help by praying. Her husband had gone out to help search. He returned about thirty minutes later with word that the boy had been found. The mother was very relieved and excitedly told her daughters the good news. One of her daughters said quite matter-of-factly, "We knew they would, Mommy. We prayed that they would." She was confident that God could and would help them find the little boy, and she wasn't at all surprised when they did.

These two true stories describe prayers that include many of the elements of effective prayer described earlier. In both cases, the approach was bold, it was made without wavering, and the request was specific. They were prayed by individuals who trusted not only that God could respond but that God would respond. The prayers involved love and compassion and were unselfish in that their purpose was tremendously beneficial to many people. The prayers were certainly expectant in nature and were very effective.

We need to recognize that God is in position to handle effectively every item that comes into His hands. We also need to recognize that God needs to be given full reign in our life. He wants to orchestrate our every move. When we let Him reign, we are offered release from the tendency to worry. When we truly let go, He takes responsibility for seeing that our lives measure up to His standards. After unconditionally surrendering our will to His, our part in this assignment is to listen intently to whatever He is saying so we will be in position to respond. We need to remember that there is absolutely no problem beyond the realm of His ability to provide a solution that will bring us peace while glorifying Himself. It is absolutely thrilling to hear the still small voice of God speaking softly but clearly, offering direction for our daily journey with Him.

FAITH

God wants our undeniable faith. *"Now faith is the substance of things hoped for, the evidence of things not seen"* (Hebrews 11:1). We do not have to take His word in blind faith due the tremendous evidence of His continuing presence. He tells us in Hebrews 11:6, *"But without faith, it is impossible to please Him, for he who comes to God must believe that He is, and that He is a rewarder of those who diligently seek Him."*

THE LIFE THAT PRAYS

To be an effective prayer warrior, it is essential to live the Christ-centered life and to let it show. Mathew 5:16 says, *"Let your light so shine before men that they may see your good works and glorify your Father in heaven."* Intercessory prayer is one of life's greatest opportunities. In surrendering to God all that we are, we find a peace and joy in life and a love for our fellowman that creates within us a deep concern for others. We cannot be isolationists. We are a vital part of the body of Christ and need to constantly reflect that we are walking not in our own power but in the strength of our Lord and Savior. Psalm 27:1 tells us, *"The Lord is my light and my salvation; whom shall I fear? The Lord is the strength of my life; of whom shall I be afraid?"* Colossians 2:6 tells us further, *"As you, therefore, have received Christ Jesus the Lord, so walk in Him."* As we stay in God's word, our prayer life will become increasingly more enjoyable and effective.

UTILIZING SCRIPTURE

Utilizing Scripture in prayer is very important. To know Scripture helps us to get to know our Heavenly Father more intimately. When we pray Scripture, we are not trying to remind God what He has promised. He never forgets anything. Instead, we are reminding ourselves of the character of the One to whom we are praying and also of His wonderful promises none of which He has ever failed to keep. Take time to focus on Scripture memorization. You will find this a refreshing aid in improving your prayer life.

THE LORD'S PRAYER

⁓

L et us take a few minutes to examine the Lord's Prayer as found in Luke 11:2-4, utilizing the aspects of effective prayer that we have just discussed. *"Our Father in heaven, hallowed be Your name, Your kingdom come, Your will be done on earth as it is in heaven. Give us day by day our daily bread, and forgive us our sins, for we also forgive everyone who is indebted to us, and do not lead us into temptation, but deliver us from the evil one."* We find included an approach to God that is respectful and a personal salutation followed by an appropriate exaltation. Also present is recognition of the existence of His heavenly kingdom as well as an expressed desire to be in His will (that the Kingdom come). There is a specific request for daily sustenance. Then, there is an acknowledgement of sinfulness with a request for forgiveness, and finally, there is recognition of His ability to keep us from Satan's grasp.

MY PERSONAL PRAYER LIFE

In my own prayer life, I like to rise early in the morning to enjoy the uninterrupted quietness. After gratefully acknowledging the presence and power of His wonderful Holy Spirit, assuring me that I will not be alone for one moment of the day, I give thanks for my many blessings.

1) I give thanks that *"The Lord is righteous in all His ways, gracious in all His works. The Lord is near to all who call upon Him, to all who call upon Him in truth"* (Psalm 145:17-18*).*

2) I acknowledge my sins and shortcomings and ask His forgiveness. Then I thank Him for being forgiving. (1 John 1:9).

3) I ask that He help me "to set my mind on things above and not on things on the earth" (Colossians 3:2).

4) I thank Him for daily benefits. "Blessed be the name of the Lord who daily loads us with benefits, even the God of our *salvation"* (*Psalm 68:19 KJV*).

5) I also like to give thanks for the fact that "The Lord God is a sun and shield; the Lord will give grace and glory; no good thing will He withhold from those who walk uprightly" (Psalm 84:11).

6) I thank Him also for His having "delivered us from the power of darkness and conveyed us into the kingdom of the Son of His love" (Colossians 1:13).

7) I then ask Him to "Direct my steps by Your word and let no iniquity have dominion over me" (Psalm 119:133).

8) I ask His assistance in allowing me to "let His word be a lamp unto my feet and a light unto my path" (Psalm 119:105).

9) From there, I go to Ephesians 6 and begin with verse 10 (*"Finally, my brethren, be strong in the Lord and the power of His might."*) This is where I prayerfully put on the full Gospel Armor. These Scripture verses provide a special strength and are wonderful verses to memorize.

Following this period of preparation with the appropriate attitude of gratitude, I move into speaking with Him about many things. As I lift my prayers to Him, I enjoy envisioning His reaching out to touch the objects of my prayers.

MAINTAINING A PRAYER JOURNAL

I t is important to maintain a prayer journal. A prayer journal is simply a way to record prayer requests and answers received. I have separate categories for different groups of people and different types of prayers. Some of these are: The church staff, the church workers and teachers, missionaries, cancer patients, people who are bereaved, people who anticipate surgery or are recovering from surgery, persons with various illnesses, those with marital, emotional, and economic problems, back-sliders, and those who are not saved. How you categorize your prayers is up to you. However, by doing so, it will help you to be more effective in your prayer life. It will help you to ensure people and requests are not forgotten. It will also serve as a wonderful reminder of God's faithfulness as answered prayers are recorded.

In conclusion, a good prayer life will strengthen your faith and draw you closer to our Heavenly Father. James 4:8a says, *"draw near to God, and He will draw near to you."* Be sure to set aside a time each day to talk with the Father. Jesus spent time in prayer each day. The Bible tells us in Mark 1:35, *"Now in the morning, having risen a long while before daylight, He went out and departed to a solitary place; and there He prayed."* Early in the morning while the mind is fresh and clear, and before Satan has had time to get a person off track, is an excellent time to pray. I can assure you that Satan will try to occupy you with other thoughts and priorities while hoping that the day will be consumed in other activities. However, we must not let him have control. When he has brought you into a mood of prayerlessness, simply force yourself to your knees, and in the name of Jesus, who soundly defeated him on the cross, order him away from you declaring that he has no control over you. Then pray. The evening is a good time to reflect upon the goodness and mercy of the Lord and to give Him thanks for His direction and blessings. When you set a time to meet Him, not only will He be expecting you, but you will certainly develop an eagerness to meet Him. I pray that the contents of this little book will enhance your prayer life and your Christian walk and be beneficial as you go to the King of Kings and the Lord of Lords.

- End -

SUMMARY - The ABC's of Effective Prayer attempts to be a simple and practical tool for helping to teach people to "*pray as they ought*" (Romans 8:26). Being the most important form of worship, it is essential for people to learn how to better communicate with the "*Giver of every good gift and every perfect gift*" (James 1:17). Some essentials are presented here in an effort to make prayer life more exciting and meaningful as we daily continue in increasingly intensified Spiritual Warfare. This is a companion book to His Word –Our Armor published in 2005.

ABOUT THE AUTHOR

B.T. PRINCE, JR., a retired businessman is an elder and outreach volunteer at Carmel Baptist Church, Matthews, North Carolina. He is also a lay minister and a lay evangelist. As a boy, faced with the death of his beloved mother, he went to the Lord in sincerity and truth, and the Lord spared her life. She was a very meaningful part of his life until she went on to be with the Lord in 1976 at the age of eighty-four. Even though very frail in her last years with her thoughts not always in tune with reality, she never closed out a day without getting on her knees. Trouble comes to all, but through prayer, a solution is available for every problem.

Printed in the United States
201075BV00004B/37-138/A

9 781600 343681